THE SAFETY OF SMALL THINGS

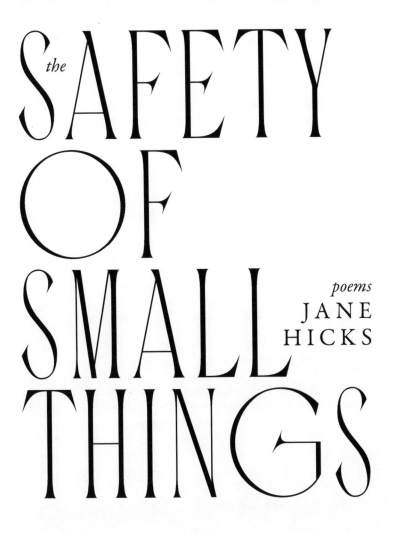

the SAFETY OF SMALL THINGS

poems
JANE HICKS

FIRESIDE INDUSTRIES

Published by Fireside Industries
An imprint of the University Press of Kentucky

Editorial and Sales Offices: The University Press of Kentucky
663 South Limestone Street, Lexington, Kentucky 40508-4008
www.kentuckypress.com

Library of Congress Cataloging-in-Publication Data

Names: Hicks, Jane, 1952– author.
Title: The safety of small things : poems / Jane Hicks.
Other titles: Safety of small things (Compilation)
Description: Lexington, Kentucky : Fireside Industries, 2024.
Identifiers: LCCN 2023041540 (print) | LCCN 2023041541 (ebook) |
    ISBN 9781950564361 (cloth ; acid-free paper) | ISBN 9781950564378 (paperback;
    acid-free paper) | ISBN 9781950564392 (adobe pdf) | ISBN 9781950564385 (epub)
Subjects: LCGFT: Poetry.
Classification: LCC PS3608.I279 S24 2024 (print) | LCC PS3608.I279 (ebook) |
    DDC 811/.6—dc23/eng/20230929
LC record available at https://lccn.loc.gov/2023041540
LC ebook record available at https://lccn.loc.gov/2023041541

For Suzanne, Patsy, and Susan
My bosom buddies

And for Wanona, who left too soon

The world is full of magic things,
patiently waiting for our senses to grow sharper.

—W. B. YEATS

Contents

Into Night

The season of cold begins with the
fire of leaves, the whisper of
ghosts. My friend has gone, a flame
against the frost extinguished.
Bright light against the alone
diminished, then winked out
like a guttered candle.

I.

The Unseen

Ten days in a drug-induced coma, Mother
plays cards with the unseen. Her fingers hold,
shuffle, and release across the pale blanket, blued
by streetlights through gaps in the shade.

Over and over, her hands repeat motions her
misfired brain feeds her fingers,
scoop, and deal again. She swats hands
that prick fingers to count blood sugar,
check for lines and needles, yet does not wake
or know we wait for her to fold,
stand pat, or open her raven eyes to fix us
with the stare that never gave away the cards she held.

She plays on as dawn rouges the blanket,
hallways stir with the clatter of carts,
not rubbered shoes of night, and the games play out.
All the while, bathed, unhooked, and tethered again,
vitals taken, bags emptied and exchanged,
she deals her tattered deck.

Spotlight
November 23, 2016

Under the one pink light of
an ultrasound room, my day
took an outlandish turn.

I clutch a gel-sodden towel over my breasts.
The lone light becomes spotlight, as if
scripted stage direction. The doctor,
young and earnest, enters,
hands me a dry towel, averts his eyes.
I re-cover. He takes my free hand,
delivers bad news: a tumor, small,
at eleven o'clock, very suspicious,
biopsy urgent. He walked over
from the hospital late on this
afternoon before Thanksgiving to spare
his nurse a grim task.

Scheduled and released, I huddle
in my car, take stock, cancel my shopping,
cancel thanksgiving, crank up music
and drive, and drive, and drive.

Safe Route

Teacher wheeled the big reel-to-reel projector, showed
that cartoon we often saw on Saturday mornings—Bert the Turtle
ducked and covered to save himself from the bomb. We practiced
the dive and crouch under our desks over and over. Outside we played
cowboys and Commies in the leaf piles at the edge of the playground,
pretended the curtains of poplar leaves breezing down to be fallout.

At my latitude, a full event not expected, but a ninety-eight percent
    eclipse.
I dug out astronomy texts, my grandson and I studied mechanics
    and revolution,
what to expect, ordered our goggles, built low-tech optics, learned
    that even
tree leaves served as shadow viewers. Our path, just outside totality,
    still a wonder.

The old wagon road winds through my acreage and down the ridge.
My neighbor described these traces of his childhood that led to nearby
farms, the store, down to the big road, some now blurred by building,
farming, and time. My walk meanders across history,
finds horseshoes uncovered after rains, across hayfields
to the tall poplars along the fencerow now embedded with barb and
    wire.

Teacher placed a purple ditto map on each desk, school at center,
a web spread from there, streets and roads on that northeast/south-
     west slant
of our hills and hollers. Each took a pencil and traced the walking
     route
home—I had a shortcut across the hayfield, aimed for the tall poplars
along the fencerow—traced it in red crayon. Red for the Commies
that would surely nuke us. This path a promise to parents where we
could be retrieved, without deviation, if the sky fell.

So difficult to fathom the nuclear furnace of the sun. How radiant,
how necessary to our life, how totality blots midday or how bright
ninety-eight percent shine might be. I learned the light would not
     be sunset-golden,
but like the verge of gloaming-silver with purple edges at moon-shadow,
the image of a moon-bitten sun would radiate through any small
     aperture,
even the space between leaves.

My favorite path on my daily route runs the edge of the ridge, a place
where two wagon roads intersect, one marked by a bent tree trunk,
said to be made by travelers on the Warriors Path, that points
down to the ancient spring and old cabin where spirits walk and wait.
I hear them speak in leaf-language.

The purpled papers yellowed and lingered on her desk as October,
November, then fifth grade passed. Eyes turned southeast to Asia,
Cuba at our feet, Communists still lurked behind every tree and fence
     post.
Autumn turned round again, the golden poplars stood like bright
     candles
on the ridge top, leaves dwindled, and Kennedy fell in Dallas. Under
     a pall,

we watched again and again as the caisson traced that same route,
without deviation, to his resting home.

The eclipse fell on a radiation day, and I waited with the staff
and other patients outside the nuclear unit. Just before maximum
  shade,
I took my turn, was radiated, joked it gave me superpowers.
Outside, we watched the sunbeam crescent shadows through shared
  glasses
and pinhole viewers. A shiny kitchen colander, held high, threw a
  hundred
bitten suns to the pavement as all silenced in that silver moment.

My summer path follows the green woods and leaf-rustle, the autumn
path lit red and gold, noisy with foot-crunch, squirrel scamper and
  deer
that bound away. At my corner, quiet comes, broken by crow call
and the thunk and thud of buckeye and walnut, the skitter of leaf-fall.
The sun crouches behind the far ridge, alights clouds with fire.

I follow the purpled path home, through the woods, across the
  hayfield,
under crimson clouds, toward the tall poplars on the fencerow. I
  think of
those gone autumns and the nuclear rain that never came and the
  radiation
that found my breast as the sun's furnace dimmed. I travel down
the ridge in purple light on that safe route home.

Abscission

September arced across the mountains, a warm
hay breeze swirled among the graven stones, nudged
faded oak leaves to chatter, stirred the scent of carnations
and the sharp odor of mums that rose from that patch of turned earth.

The day a mountain postcard, dogwoods rusted at woods' edge
behind the church and buckeyes blazed among the green.
For weeks, that perfect sky taunted me and turned
into October—those days that cause me to chant Yeats
as I walk the dry paths and shuffle gold with my feet.

November came to save me. The rain dripped from eaves,
felled the gaudy leaves, and closed the sky
so I could shut the windows, light the fire, and keen into my tea.

PTSD

Like a lazy serpent, drowses on a speckled path,
soaks the sun, digests a lunch,
rises to strike a careless wanderer;

a panther that stalks ridgeline,
weaves about boulders and trees, a sinuous hunger
of claws and teeth, devours frolicking young;

an undertow that lurks beneath
predictable waves, circles and roils,
waits casual wader to sweep away and drown;

a mountain storm that lashes, strikes,
and topples ancient pines onto a cabin,
a refuge thought safe.

Birthday, 1956

Already hunkered down at four,
her back to the high ground,
organza dress brushes the grass.
The gaze, blue and myopic,
stares down the camera. Her chin
rests on fists with bitten nails.

The hand-tinted enlargement
paints the dress a mendacious blue
to match the eyes. The fluff of ruffled
trim shows a white print with
patterns of strawberries, the true
dress a red and scratchy memory.

Black patents and ruffled socks
peek from beneath, the socks denuded
later that day with her blunt tip scissors,
the crinoline dropped behind a lilac bush.

She already knows what lies
behind the lens, the candy stripes
her legs will wear for damage done.

The wind lifts the sunlit ponytail
at camera click and calls to her.
She listens to the power lines sing

on the hill, follows them away
to the world and work of words
where brushstrokes do not lie.

Shine

Sometimes there comes a crack in Time itself.

S. V. BENÉT

Think about history—
when and where Time cracked.
What fell through?
Did Time refocus, shift path askew,
or beam onward?
Gravity bends light; light can focus, break apart
to wave and particle, slowed
in dark laboratories, measured in minute
bursts on arcane instruments. Perhaps Time bends.
Einstein called humans "slowed down sound and light waves,"
noted that we walk in "biochemical garments."

Pay attention!
Do cracks break open and scatter Time
or does a beam bore through focused?
It's possible cracked Time depends
on the break and its nature
be it jagged or clean-broken.
Einstein's dreamed beam that bore him across this universe
perhaps a Time-cracked gift. Give thanks he paid attention,
who might receive that understanding? Anyone? No one?
Our loss?

Look up!
Find gifts that might pass unnoticed.

Know we may have fallen, like angels or demons,
through the first crack in Time.
We walk electric in our sparking garments,
look down, believe dogma, so easy,
no thought to challenge our now.
Galileo knew what moved. Stood firm—
Earth not omphalos, not navel of this universe—
It moved.

Push!
Find Time cracks, universal shifts
in light and energy.
Expect gifts.

Shine!

The Dark

The beast of winter, still fat
on apples and meat, winds through
the trees, moans, wails, rattles
branches, calls down snow and ice.
Furry feet pad and crackle on the
porch, on the roof, huddle
beneath the eaves, hang icicles.
The beast howls on, becomes lean,
outrageous in his shadowing of the sun,
goes to ground. Becomes food for
buds and blossoms on swelled branches.

Agent of Providence

Roma Downey glows on the television screen,
her angel touch dispensed, the plotline closed.
I have muted the sound as my mother drifts toward sleep.
We shiver in the bare, temporary room where she has come
for transfusion. I drowse over my coffee.
It's not like that, she declares.
I rouse, arch an eyebrow in response.
Angels. She gestures toward the TV as
her IV tubes arc out and glitter. *Not at all.*

She ought to know. My mother once died
and went to Heaven. In a coma for three weeks,
one long night set off bells and alarms in the ICU.
She told anyone who would listen that she ascended
through pink clouds that smelled of roses to meet Jesus,
who she assured us would nowadays be detained
at any airport, looked nothing like in Sunday school.
She asked if she had gained Heaven.
Jesus promised her it would be whatever she desired
paradise to be, but not yet. He sent her home,
"You're not done suffering yet."

*Angels brought me back. Big scary angels with nary
a feather in sight. People have it wrong
when they show pretty women and fat baby angels.
Was anybody in the Bible glad to see angels? Mostly not;*

Jacob wrestled his, Sarah laughed at hers, Lot's scared
him enough to flee Sodom dragging his family. Mary met
Gabriel, that poor little girl. Just imagine. The shepherds
in Bethlehem were sore afraid. Them angels in the lion's den
and fiery furnace weren't fellows to mess with, no,
or the one set at the gates of Eden with a sword of flame.

She falls back into meds and sleeps. I study
angels on my phone, find that only
cherubim and seraphim sprout wings.
I ponder archangels, find Gabriel and Michael,
learn Raphael and Uriel of the flaming sword.
The Kabbalah names seven: one with the glorious
name Metatron, fit for a superhero.

We, created less than the angels, reduced them,
rendered them as harp-wielding and infantile.
Should I, like the psalmist, call on angels for help,
I want a being who can stand in the presence of God,
who bears a sword, or commands a voice like a lion,
to be the agent of Providence and the harbinger of grace.

Caesura

Dawn lifts, pulls a yellow morning
into view, breeze mingles treetops,
red-tailed hawk wheels and drafts,
worried by crows until
he plummets, plucks a vole
from a dew-wet meadow, retreats to feed.
Vultures slow-circle possum splayed
on gravel road where children
trudge to a bus, wrinkle noses as they pass.
Driver waits, watches white crane wade
pond's edge, spear its breakfast,
lift its head to swallow.

Mam Recounts Family History

Holland? I could scarce credit our family to be
low-landers, perched here on this canted ridge.
"Granny made clear they sailed from Holland.
Sewed corpses in sails and dropped them over
the side when a scourge hit the boat and her
old granny left a widow."

Armed with my Mam's conviction,
memories, and a few names,
I scoured the genealogy stacks of musty
documents, foxed-edge papers, and leather-
bound books to be handled with white gloves.

I found them in the Minutes of the Friends,
my Quaker ancestors, not four generations back,
but twenty. They fled from England to Holland,
to Barbados, half-dead from fever,
then shipwrecked, her old granny widowed,
toting a baby, stunned at Providence and His plan.
The ship turned toward the Carolinas. No family
alive, she sailed back to London and
took up a new religion.

But the boy looked west
all his youth, shipped back to Carolina to found
our line. Start the story again of the ship from

Holland that ended on a ridge in Tennessee.
Those Quakers turned Brethren, turned Baptists,
all English, not Dutch. The shipwrecked boy
washed up on a mountain, to land that called him back.

This Morning, in the Mist

A hawk wings
climbs, seeks
thermals, wheels,
bathes in breeze
no hunt
desire to be lifted

out over the valley
a curtain of rain
awash in summer
no prey below
but hawk hunger
to glide and float.

The Time I Stole

On parched summer days, my precious six weeks
of non-teacher days, my boys would not venture
into the inferno, sought the cool, knew
they were forbidden entrance to my "office"
at writing time. Toes on the threshold,
my acrobats tilted forward, bodies near-parallel
to the floor, into my room of books and spells
tapped out on an old IBM Selectric, demanded
I come out and play or feed the grubby troupe.

Now, my husband, not so acrobatic or trainable,
stampedes through my poems, my mother rings
and rings, leaves no message until I pick up
and speak. On workdays, among graded papers
and monthly federal reports, nothing is amiss
if I write at my desk while students wander the maze
of the paragraph. A principal once commended
this model of desired behavior. It was time I stole,
a string of words heard at a faculty meeting,
that troubled and tangled my concentration,
if not tied to the paper with haste.

Dancing in the Stars

She made her last wishes interspersed with commentary
about *Dancing with the Stars*. We acted as critics
on footwork, hair, barely-there costumes,
and the general stupidity of voting fans.

"I want 'Where the Roses Never Fade' played at my funeral,
sung by the Sego Brothers and Naomi," she remarked
just after a spirited paso doble. After a dreamlike waltz,
she continued, "Bury me in that nightgown and robe
you got me for Christmas. Pull a fuzzy blanket over me.
I'm going to my rest, not to town." She focused
on the firm posterior of a handsome Russian in full
cha-cha mode. "I won a jitterbug contest once.
I wore shocking pink."
She demanded bright flowers, not pale pastels, for her casket.
Not pausing a beat, she ordered me to write down the
voting number for her favorite dancers.

She lay in state wearing cherry pink,
covered by a fuzzy throw, warm socks on her ever-cold feet.
A flurry of calls found Naomi never recorded that song—
confirmed by Naomi herself—a suitable replacement found.
September's palette topped her casket: purple, crimson,
gold, orange, and scarlet, ribbons bedecked with sequins.
Come spring, I returned to tidy

the grave and give a rundown on last night's show,
not caring what an observer would think
as I jitterbugged to the car.

Pocket Money

to Wanona

She limps, leans heavy on the cane as we circle
the rec room. One chemo took her jaw,
another took her ankle, not enough bone to hold a pin,
yet the cancer swims through, dies down, returns.
We pass a pool table and she swings the cane up,
banks a perfect shot to the pocket, leaves the cue ball
in place to run the table. Her turbaned head tilts,
I catch the rogue in her that hustled the guys
in the student union for pocket money. She suckered them
in her low-slung jeans, all big eyes and auburn braids,
pretended to be taught well enough to bet them a game.
Then, I retrieved her custom cue from behind my chair,
and she mowed them down as they learned their lesson,
the one about thinking with the wrong head,
thinking she was just a girl. She has suckered death,
thus far. I held her hand five years ago when they gave
her a few months. Her body will go to science but death
will have to beat her hustle. Like then, I can only watch,
hope death will be her mark and time her pocket money.

Night Music

I roll down windows and fly
through honeysuckle nights,
radio replays my youth,
nights WOWO came
through after midnight, oldies
a comfort of a well-worn quilt.
Breakups, meltdowns, high school
drama, dances that sent us into crisp autumn
sweat-soaked, long hair damp curtains,
songs that had dance names morphed
into protest as my senior year rolled round.
I dreamed of escape to college,
decade turned: Motown, acid rock,
protest, Jimi Hendrix, Janis Joplin,
a rough world, classmates called
to war. We thought not to survive
the Cuban Missile Crisis, seed for hippies
that seized any day that might be their last.
I drive on past drowsy cows,
wary of bounding deer, stop at mountain
overlook under a blackberry sky
to watch stars herded across dark heavens—
Hercules treads on Draco,
Littlest Dipper overhead,
the Lyre of Heaven strums across the night.

Ode on an Onion

Neruda declared *under the earth, the miracle happened.*
The onion ball grew in dark, a world within a world,
within a world, layer by layer until harvest, tight
golden skin, still green tops, and dangling root hairs,
a cool, luminous moisture laid to rest in dry sun.

Neruda missed knowing secrets my grandmother
taught me of this tiny world. How petals
made a poultice for a rattling chest or astringent
for a festered cut. How fried with lard and potatoes
we staved off hunger in the long cold. How papery
skins wrapped about eggs, boiled with vinegar,
brought forth treasures for Easter hiding, or soft yellow
wool boiled in enamel pans over a wood fire.

Neruda sang of ephemeral shapes,
transparencies, and tears. I sing of a miracle
that grew in black creek bottoms, dried in sun,
kept in a root cellar, brought forth
to granny's table in half-light of winter
and her medical trove to carry sun's gold.

Persimmons

Our old house has doubled its size and the street paved.
Beyond, the ridge remains, giant poplars on the tree line,
furrowed hollows that run down to the river.

The persimmon trees have multiplied and grown strong,
a whole childhood of play in the rings around,
year after year. A prank for city cousins,
green, astringent, lockjaw-bitter, sweet treat for
the short days after frost, magnets for night
creatures that spread the seeds round the ridge,
ammunition for the witch who cursed us from
her immaculate porch, our only transgression youth.
Under cover of darkness, we rode over the tree and released
it and its fruit to the blank canvas of pristine house and yard.

She died alone. Her distant kin care not, the house
stands ready for auction, the faint stains rusty
beneath a faded coat of white. Broken pots hold no
blooms, a fountain dry, its angel of broken wings grounded,
boarded windows mute where no music ever played.
The garden that fed her now feeds deer and groundhogs
with volunteer crops, weeds choke the flower beds,
and persimmons sprout along the footers.

II.

Notes from the Forgotten Year

Advised to keep a journal,
I wondered how one could
forget this thing, this cancer.
But I wrote the details.
I examined the pages after,
sad and astounded by forgotten
details of that long year.

1.

Flipped through
Southern Living, People,
old travel magazines
about places I didn't want to go.
Just a routine call back,
image splotched, reshoot.
Planned shopping after.
Routine on its head.

Held a gel-soaked towel
over suspect breast,
ultrasound tech
called radiology,
earnest doctor walked over
from hospital

to tell me *It's not good,*
but it's small,
lymph nodes look clear.

Breathed deep,
breathed slow,
alone in my car,
pondered it all,
low risk, except age.
No lump, no sign,
just a dark spot
where last year was none.
Shock, denial,
cranked up music.
I drove curvy
back roads home.

Waited for call
to schedule biopsy,
searched out surgeons,
oncologists,
searched Internet,
got scared. Breathed
like they taught me
for childbirth.

Wrote Christmas cards,
waited for biopsy day,
answered questions on nurse's call,
fought urge to Google,
remembered friend who died,
took a breath,
called nurse advocate,

got a recording.
Hello. Hello.

Waited for biopsy.
Hurt like hell,
off-kilter,
wobbled to waiting room,
ice pack in bra, home,
slept it off,
saw grandkids,
faked normal.
Faked calm.

Phone in hand,
ductal carcinoma in situ,
invasive, small,
high grade, fast growing.
Told husband,
took another call,
scheduled surgeon on Monday,
decided who and what to tell.
Kept breathing.

2.

Surgeon's office,
husband and friend supported,
pathology report, explanation,
I froze, unlikely self-silence, stunned,
one report lacking.
Lumpectomy scheduled
next week, after Christmas.
I heard excellent prognosis.

Decided who to tell,
ruin Christmas for kids,
brother, and chosen family.
Waited last pathology report,
took a trip, bucket list item filled,
talked with friend who had it worse,
good info,
started a journal.
New perspective.

Pre-op session,
saw bright screen
tracking patients' progress,
imagined myself
in a few days,
a color-coded
number on a screen.
Filled out color-coded forms,
answered questions,
no family history,
not one soul.

Cooked Christmas dinner,
opened gifts,
kissed grandchildren,
played and laughed, good music.
Saw side glances of grown children.
Kept smiling.

Two days before surgery,
decided to busy myself,
wrote letters to friends,
tried to stay offline,

failed.
Researched side effects
and outcomes,
went to tai chi,
cleaned up Christmas.

3.

Women's Center,
procedure before surgery,
unwarned of needles and wires,
shot in nipple, shock, trembles, terror.
Surgery Center for tender care,
women's hands soothed.

Sipped soda, nibbled crackers,
clear vision, drug stupor, kind nurse,
remembered crawling on table,
warm blankets, soft hands,
rose up to wakeful.
Dressed, walked to husband,
to car. Lumpectomy over.

Sore, bandaged, groggy,
slept less and less,
bandages off,
stitches, aches,
bruises, dents and dimples,
slept without pain.
Better and better, read, wrote.
Call comes.
Margins clear!

Surgeon checkup,
cosmesis good, feel stronger,
expect radiation schedule,
more pathology done,
treat as triple negative.
Strike three,
got a dance with the Red Devil,
advised to take no chances,
oncologist appointment,
change of direction.
Chemo.
Dance with the Devil.
Dance for my life.

Waited for oncologist,
did paperwork,
always paperwork,
tuned out television,
resisted inauguration ruckus.
Efficient doctor,
facts, figures, data,
confirmation
of what my gut told me,
survival data, side effects,
one year dedicated to battle,
a deployment.
I would fight.

Chair of my friend,
longtime hairdresser,
my hair on floor,
stylish, pixie short.
My pockets

buzzed and rang,
dates set,
port, chemo,
prescriptions ready,
my face large in mirror,
age showed,
stripped down for battle.

4.

Surgery center redux,
female staff, sympathetic,
remembered my lumpectomy.
More anesthesia,
woke with chemo port
underneath collarbone,
hooked in skin to vein.
Drowsy, new portal ached.
Veins opened.

Lounge chair, heat, vibrated,
curtained from others,
new port waited, needle ready,
friend and husband anxious,
waited, guts twisted.
A nurse brought
red bag in a red bag,
port attached to line,
in it went, red as blood,
raced through,
raced through,
a train not stopped,
handled with goggles,

with gloves,
put it in me.
I began the dance.

Lady barber buzz-cut my tufts,
most gone in shower that day,
GI Jane now, badass,
stared down mirror,
scant week later,
lint roller pulled away rest.

No hair
on legs, arms, pits, pubes,
I looked ten,
minus stretch marks and baby pouch,
my arms bare, goose-bumped,
more naked than birth, when
at least I had a tonsured fringe.
Brows and lashes remained,
soon gone.
No one told me about
nose hair, gone,
I sniffed like a coke addict,
bent forward,
I dripped like the IV they hung
every other week.

Stumbled, missed chair,
broke my favorite mug.
Bathed in coffee,
stomach revolted,
too dizzy for shower,

mourned mug, head swam.
Body broken.

Devil Dance done,
stomach settled, head cleared,
a break given, got away.
Ocean backed out like crab,
tide fell, breeze salty,
a rhythm, breath slowed,
shrimp smelled good,
food called.

5.

Taxol hung,
reaction team ready,
drip, drip,
wait, wait,
five minutes gone,
ten minutes gone.
Nurse smiled,
wheeled away
unneeded crash cart,
Benadryl kicked in,
drip continued.
Eleven more drip times.

Knees and hips pulsed
like beacons,
imagined I saw orange hot pain,
arthralgia mentioned
in passing arrived.

Sit, stand, walk, all hurt.
Tried to read,
chemo brain lost trail
of plot and details.
Poetry endures.
Ignored orange pulse,
planned what to do
with "my one life."

That same room,
pink tie-front gown,
same magazines,
floral upholstery, soft colors,
locker key on my wrist,
six months gone
since tumor excised.
I waited, imagined the worst.
Technician, same technician,
prepared me,
dropped my sleeve,
sticky markers for scar,
pressure, pressure,
held breath, waited.
Side, middle, side,
her work methodical.
Mammogram done.

Walking hurt,
toes, feet numb, prickled,
zinged electric.
I waddled,
feet didn't relay

what lay underneath,
uneven ground diabolical.
I would have sworn my feet
rounded and swelled
as softballs,
eyes said different.
Numb, tingle, burn.
Stumble.

Needle snapped into port,
steroid injected into line,
Taxol hung.
Benadryl took over,
I drowsed,
blood pressure
every fifteen minutes,
roused, drowsed,
IV beeped, beeped, beeped.
I dripped my last.
Chemo over,
fatigued, foot-numbed,
I stumbled out,
rang bell.

6.

Met radiologist,
confirmed my plan,
saw machines,
learned the lingo,
heard rare side effects,
confirmed The Plan.

Another table,
stretched back, exposed,
imprint formed, mold cast
for my bombardment,
radiation coordinates marked,
skin pricked,
tattoos inked for alignment,
for the great eye that lowered,
hummed, winked, glittered
as a thousand slots adjusted
to my tattooed coordinates,
permanent reminders
marked.

Looked long at life,
numbered those
who stayed and stood,
dropped ones who fled,
abandoned friendships, kinship,
learned this loss was common.
Heard others retell tales
of abandonment,
wondered at human weakness.

Grassy bank
with radiation staff and patients,
solar glasses, homemade viewers,
some in scrubs, some gowned,
to view eclipse.
Appointed time, each went in,
got radiated, came back out.
Light dimmed,
trees cast silvered shadows

on hot pavement, tiny suns.
Light winked out,
we gasped as one.
Who winks next?
We are stardust.

Chatted with Suzanne, Susan, Patsy,
waited to radiate,
compared hair growth,
color, texture,
sorority and sympathy
five days a week,
two hopeful, two anxious,
joked that we four
had three boobs between us.

After the eclipse
that August day,
I inquired of the doctor
if it gave superpowers.
No, he laughed.
Sobered, he said—
you already have them,
you women.

Looked at same art,
metal floral sculpture,
poster-sized photos.
TV never on in women's
waiting area,
always on in men's,
vibrating wall between.
Patsy came out,

Susan arrived,
Suzanne left,
I went in.
These six weeks,
these twenty-five days,
became bosom buddies,
laughed at that joke,
exchanged numbers,
Suzanne gifted identical bracelets.
We finished.
Sisters by fire,
burned and blistered breasts
initiation in our sorority.

7.

Nowhere to go,
nothing on calendar.
A sudden halt
of attention
to my body,
shock, suspension.
Withdrawal from action.
Needed debriefing.

That same room,
soft green wallpaper,
lavender shades, mood light,
pink tie-front gown.
One year ago,
breast betrayed.
Now scarred and carved,

my armpit numbered, marked,
nipple and one breast darker
than other, I waited.
Annual diagnostic.
Treatment tale told
in bright lines on dark film.
Scarred and scared.

A paper cape,
awaited surgeon,
mammogram results.
A year ago, she said
breast could be saved.
Breast saved,
twice poisoned.
Radiated until
nipple blistered and peeled.
Immune system
cranked and crashed.
Surgeon spoke:
Clear.

Thought of that day,
a year ago,
world spun out of control,
second bad mammogram,
worse ultrasound,
on that day before Thanksgiving.

My breast now healed,
my head clearing
of chemical fog,

my calendar empty of doctors.
I gave thanks.
Closed the journal, rose,
and walked on.

Closed Hold

Everyone holds a story.
Not everyone tells a story.

Not everyone tells a story,
buried deep, reached but by nightmare.

Buried deep, reached but by nightmare,
fists, wasps of words, forbidden doors opened.

Fists, wasps of words, forbidden doors opened,
shadows in gloom, hand across the mouth,

Shadows in gloom, hand across the mouth,
stranger, kin, false friend—power and control.

Stranger, kin, false friend—power and control.
Heart bruise and flesh wounds heal and fade.

Heart bruise and flesh wounds heal and fade,
leave storied scars we every one hold.

Shadows

A human can appear in light
to possess beauty of movement, face,
a perfection of nature. But each time
night fell, our doors shut, I learned
the dark shows truth, brings forth
snakes and vermin, sly movement
with slitted eyes, furtive and quick.

Drop a white hood
over beauty, in the dark, and see
smoky flames reveal festering hate.

I know, learned young, hate hides
its face in unexpected places.
I learned to watch in the dark,
never surprised at things discovered.

Lair

That moment you spy that snake
in the garden and know it for a liar.
Beautiful and cunning, its tricky tongue
keeps you in your place. The flowers, fruits,
and wild tangle part, illusion dispelled,
cunning lair revealed.

Too busy dodging fists, curses, threats
that swarm your head to see filth that lies
at your feet, mire of lies, deflection
of purpose. You catch him, stare him down,
plan your escape.

What I Learned

The secret life

begins early . . .

BILLY COLLINS

I learned a lot in school. Oh, I know,
we all did, but I learned that some daddies
left for work and came home every day.
That some daddies hugged and kissed children,
helped with homework, and declared
their children beautiful and smart.

I learned that not all daddies had a white robe
and peaked hood in the trunk of their cars, or
that many children were driven in their daddies'
cars, not locked out.

I learned that some daddies laughed
with their children, played games.
My friends' daddies went to PTA
instead of cursing it as meddlesome,
and some daddies even sat and talked
without swearing or preaching about Communists.

I learned some daddies drank too much, some daddies
never came back. Some daddies had belts and switches,
but never left welts and cuts to keep a child from school.
Some daddies woke crying from war dreams, but arose
to take children to church.

I learned, at school, by listening, that a daddy
most often was a good thing
and I learned to be sad.

Mississippi, 1964

Tailgate riders windblown to relief
from Mississippi summer rode daily
to the general store near the bayou.

Paw's carpenter hands, generous
on our biannual visits, passed
jingles for MoonPies, Orange Nehi,

cheese and crackers on the front porch.
Done farming and logging for the day,
sun-brown men whittle and spit

in the gravel and bottle caps out front,
wish on the weather, talk trotlines
and other matters in a hush with cautious

eyes cast our direction upon litanizing
Black folks, outside agitators, and meetings.
The summer of 1964, my twelfth,
gleamed hottest and Mississippi burned

with, for, and because of freedom.
Paw left us on the other end of the porch;
white-hot conversation swarmed the group

like angry yellow jackets, rose to fury
by store-close at dark. Paw stayed
near that night, one of us either side

the porch swing, eyes on the black highway.
The road ran busy the next two months
with endless columns of green soldiers.

The last day of our visit, a khaki
parade marched up from the back pasture,
parted cattle like the Red Sea to deliver three

who, like Shadrach, Meshach, and Abednego, refused
bowing to tradition, unlike them, burned for truth;
body bags evident as the convoy passed.

We left Mississippi, home to blue hills.
Walter Cronkite narrated what I saw,
expressed what I could not. Child words

too small for the woeful, awful knowledge
burned into me by the Mississippi sun.
Cooled only by the fact Paw
stayed home the night innocence died.

Haiku

Thirty-seven turkeys graze
grubs, acorns, beechnuts,
slick, autumn-bright, rain-glazed.

Take This Leaf

... read these leaves in the open air every season of every year of your life...
WALT WHITMAN

Open to air and sky, one feels none other
than small, a particle, a part, a leaf, a blade of a great whole.
Feel the rustle, stir, and hum as all moves together,
give and get cycles of earth, air, sun, and water.
The bob of flower heads as bees lift away,
whir of hummingbird wing, feather that floats to earth.
All binds. The moth wing sets
waves in motion, a mountain's face peels away,
slides to its feet. A sigh upon leaves,
a gift returned, sweat on a brow, rain anew.
The sun, a lamp, a hearth, what needs be
when needs be. Small. All crouch small
beneath the vault of the sky, or held in the bowl
of the mountains, washed in light,
flow out free where science and soul meet.

Longing

Buddha taught that *dukkha,* anxiety and stress,
come from wanting. The desire to cling
to impermanent things prevents our revels and peace.
One wants a mirror that does not change,
a child that does not grow, a sunset that does
not bleed into the bruise of night, an autumn
that clings to the tired trees and robs them of rest.

Change is the journey; "let evening come," said the poet.
Let life come and unfold: flowered field, purple evenings,
withered flesh, cold stones. Consider the lilies of the apostle Luke,
let go the hornets of worry, bathe in the stream of life.

Jack Higgs Walks Alone at Hindman

In the morning backlight, the scholar ambles
stage left, discovering along the path
to the James Still Building, stops to touch
the Yellow Rain Tree, deadhead the marigolds,
admire the tumble of stone hearth and chimney
abandoned below the steep bank.

Surrounded always by supplicants,
this lone sighting from my high window
needs note. Sun clears the shadows from Pushback Ridge,
lights his silver aura amidst the deep green.
Trees block his exit right, leaves me to wonder
and vision his path, ever the pilgrim.

Kept Things

My grandmother's tin shears hang
above my sewing machine, a rusted reprimand.
Too big for my hand, they remind me of real work.
Never meant for fabric, she employed them
for every task, barring flimsy goods:
repair a roof, cut flowers, bailing twine,
corduroy, or chicken wire. Her shears
one of two weapons of defense in a perilous world,
the other a hoe, blood-sharp,
edge flashing as she scratched weeds
from her potential larder, a walking stick, a dispatch
for serpents with whack and swoosh as they flew to weeds,
her progress on the row or path never halted.
A chipped crock still wears a rusted wire that bound
oil cloth over brown sugar, to keep out ants and small fingers,
now holds napkins or silverware for a buffet.
My mother's Bible storybook kept, not just to trace her
childish hand, but to touch things my women touched,
see vain repair, and instructions to bear
her world in ways no longer borne, to know her confusion
in the claim of herself against things she no longer need carry.

Persist

Sun-dappled drowsy fawns sprang
up at every turn of the trail last spring.
The doe deposited them, always apart,
in thickets, brush piles, honeysuckle warrens,
collected them at day's end. I often saw them
in shadows, suckled in the gloaming,
my walks timed to disturb them least until they grew
nimble, spooked less, learned to lay low.

Sleek-muscled, wary, the wood sprites, mother and daughters
still appear as three, still graze in woods'-edge dawns
and open field twilights. Fall brought forth the mother wounded,
shot across the shoulder, flesh ripped raw, fur pulled away,
spine spared. I watched, hoped she would not succumb—she
    persisted.
Spring, timid this year, finds her healed, graceful, still mother to
    beauty.

I ponder the doe, her healing given as a sign,
I persist. Chemicals course through, fog my words,
tear my hair from me, leave a specter's reflection.
The fall wounded us all on the ridge, my breast, stitched,
cancer excised, healed as the doe healed.

Pyburn Creek

Follow sun-dabbed path to the aged and infirm
sycamore that refuses to yield to years,
across creek log, upstream to that green place,
below water-cut and weathered bank.
The flow tumbles over falls built by a brother and sister
beneath pawpaw trees, black-blossomed in spring,
fragrant-fruited by summer end. Find the boulder
washed down by long-ago torrent. Perch and listen,
draw watery breath, soak in the green, the yellow,
the blue of the season. Burbles, bird calls, distant cattle,
wind whistle or whimper in weeds and briars.
Remember dinner bell of the long afternoon called
you home to porch swing, night breeze sweetened
by white blossom and a hymn on the tongue.

Safety of Small Things

Deadfall disallows glimpses and visits
with deer and woodpeckers.
The squirrels and chipmunks, near-frantic,
ignore the hiker on the path.
The fox has gone to ground.
A rain moves through.
The pin oaks rattle and branches clack;
the wind worries the ridge. On the lee side,
an inchworm measures a shelf fungus.

Here, a night nest, warm wallow
in the tall grass that edges the brush pile—
a deliberate thicket composed for the safety
of small things. Tunnels and trails,
marked by tufts of hair and feathers,
lead to an unseen world that flourishes
while I sleep.

Follow

I waved my hand
over the patch but made no shadow
in that place . . .
MAURICE MANNING

The chemo clouds and veils thought,
a stream hits a rock dam, splashes, diffused,
lost but to weeds and mud. A reader cannot read,
follow the course of thought through a chapter,
the flow of an essay, the journey of an article.
The poem saves, its brevity runs thought
to a stop, grasped, apprehended.
Reread, underline, pause, image clear,
word-echo provokes, the thought hovers, takes
form. Step-by-step, poems like creek
stones or tree-blazed marks bring one through
forest, tangled and bare, to tangled
and green after a lost winter,
underlined words a pocket of found
treasure, proof of the trail and the guide.

After Chemo #2

Mr. Clean in mascara,
lashes not yet gone but
every wrinkle, knot, and bump
exposed on the skull, eyes too large,
puffy, dark-circled, ears too small,
like an afterthought, neck long,
jaw square, no wattle,
face now floats
on its own, an exposure,
quizzical and pale, not fierce as need
be yet, will emerge from
this boot camp shock,
head up, chin out.

Neophyte

Lila B. Buchanan

1900–1995

Still ramrod straight at eighty-five, Chanel-suited,
she dodged cow piles and sharp gravel to pick
her way to a metal-flake Cadillac. The morning
lit her apricot bouffant—the remnant of auburn.
I drove her to the hulking Victorians
that dotted the farm valley roads. She led me into
elegant caves that smelled of beeswax and tea biscuits.

The bridge coven met in these caverns: chatelaines of heritage
farms, land-grant mavens of elegant pedigree. Master players
taught me the bluff, the bid, and china and silver patterns
graced with old roses, family crests, hallmarks, history,
tea service, linen. I learned Hepplewhite, Sheraton, Regency
styles from our playing tables and parlor chairs.

For my rent, I chauffeured this woman who
took me on, a project. I find her in antique stores,
holiday home tours, in myself as I spread a cloth
and lay service for guests with the things she gave me.

Tobacco

I.

The tobacco of my childhood hung whispery and dry
in the rafters. No fires or flues like in low country,
only woodsmoke drifted up from the house stove
lingered outside the work shed. The November rains,
sharp and flinty cold, brought the dried leaves into case,
pliable enough to be handled on a human assembly line
denuding long stalks of lugs, long red, bright, and tips
graded and gathered into hands—bundles tied at the top—
packed on flat wooden baskets, piled higher than our heads,
we children the proper weight to compact the crop.
Hands gummy from sap, an ever-present nicotine high
helped warm our sneakered feet on the dirt floor.

II.

Woodsmoke and dried leaves hung inside the shed
of an unfortunate first marriage. A woodstove and concrete
floor, an upgrade, my ability to tie a perfect hand of tobacco
my saving grace among people who scorned my bookish ways.
The flat baskets now head-high and packed down with weights
built for such endeavor. Hands gummy, nicotine buzz,
tobacco dust all paid tuition and student loans.
Dried leaves and woodsmoke,
the dry, the dead, and the burned.

III.

December howls outside, dried leaves and tobacco smoke
hang in the rafters of the growers' warehouse. Stand beside
crops as buyers follow auctioneer up and down long rows
of tall baskets, his chant echoes through the cavernous
tin-topped market. A bright smile might boost the price,
blond head toss and low-slung jeans sell
the nicotine buzz to buy an extra book, new tires.

IV.

Dirt floors and sheds gone, the concrete floors abandoned,
warehouses stand near-empty. I divorced the scent of
dried leaves, woodsmoke, and nicotine. Left behind
the cold work of November rain and December wind,
an enterprise centered on smoke, the dead, and dying.

An East Tennessee Parking Lot

The gull backpedals midair, cries
"dive, dive," drops to the cracked pavement.
Shoppers stare, puzzled, wind stirs
litter, and the gull rises, chases wrappers,
trash, stale scraps. She drops again,
skids across the icy parking lot,
five hundred miles from the ocean,
blown on the wind, unexpected
as this life that lifts and drops
us in some chance place.

III.

Remnants of a Saving Life

Hard things
from hard people dulled on Depression,
trenches of France, left not objets d'arte
but objects of work and care.

A pewter cup
my grandfather picked up
after it fell from a covered wagon in Texas,
1893, and the roads led west.

Cast-iron skillets
well-seasoned a hundred years,
a whiff brings dreams of bounty
cooked in a woodstove.

A bowed yardstick
fitted with a weighted brass hook,
retriever of bolted cloth shelved
in my great-uncle's store.

Shears
filled all functions—
my grandmother's hefty all-purpose
trimming tools.

A china doll
wears flapper hair, green eyes, painted shoes,
otherwise naked,
hairline crack across her torso.

Hymnbooks
taught me *fa-so-la* then
note reading for the piano.

Cedar chest
holds well-worn and new quilts,
scraps, pieces, remnants of
a saving life.

Tea set,
tiny, ages in a fragile box
marked one cent, traded
for a bucket of hulled walnuts,
treasured for eighty years.

Communion

Beneath crumbling shale banks, under low branches,
we dam Pyburn Creek. I stack pebbles along
shallows to pen crawdads my brother catches.
This spot, this shade, this creek, take up
the hottest hours before supper.

Blue mud at creek's edge smells
primeval and decayed. Crawdads escape
pen by morning and build their mounded
flood dams. A mulberry harbors squirrels,
birds, seen but not heard over creek rush.

Sycamores green water edge. Further back
grow poplars, straight-up tall, and buckeyes,
already red-leafed in August. Dogwood
berry necklaces like blood droplets in the green.
Cold, cold creek water surges and scrambles
down mountain, carries, urges,
wears stone and tree to sand and soil.

Called to supper, we bathe in a washtub
of sun-warmed creek water to cleanse our mud,
afterward douse prize dahlias in a side garden.
Tick-checked and dressed, we eat homegrown
bounty, then drowse in porch swings.

II.

Buffet on flatbed wagons, congregation
fills stiff paper plates with layers of favorites.
Feasters once spread through shady cemetery
on quilts or perched on stones among their departed,
now seek picnic tables in outdoor
shelter while an acoustic trio sings praise.

Dessert comes out last, a fancy after plain fare.
Coconut, apple stack, and yellow cake
clothed in caramel crown feast.
Chocolate, cherry, chess, and lemon pies,
banana puddings, meringued in brown peaks,
weep with heat.

After country communion, congregation walks
out among stones. They stroll, stop,
chat before monuments, reconnect
lines of kinship, adjust floral displays,
check for newcomers gone to ground,
unconscious nod to songs carried on faint breeze.

III.

Water, stone, sand and soil—
this is where we begin and end.

Drawn

I.

Walking on nerve-numbed toes
separates flesh from the earth
that comforts and teaches me on wooded paths,
once muddy farm roads, bordered with rusted wire
embedded into oak and poplar along the fence line,
trunks assaulted and scavenged by woodpeckers,
pileated nest holes in trees grown tall toward the sun
from deep ravines, eye level from my vantage
on this bare ridgetop.

II.

I sit on a patch of green, trace tree roots beneath,
taste moss and acorns with my fingers, pull back
tufts loosened by deer hoof, find shale,
watch obsidian insects scurry to cover.
Summer flutters above.
When I last walked this path,
limbs clacked and wind nipped.

III.

I lost time like a dream. Months gone while poison dripped,
excised the thing that ate me, a gall like the oak bears,

a disrupted flow. On my moss bed, shoes flung aside,
feet and fingers touch, draw from the earth.
All flows through, nourishes, heals.

Cumberland Gap above the Furnace

Gap Creek winds and crashes through a river
of boulders big as cars tumbled down the mountain.
Mosses and ferns green the banks, carpet stone,
waterfalls splash and spray. Lights dapple rock and water.

Sycamores green water edge. Further back
grow poplars, straight-up tall, and buckeyes,
already red-leafed in August. Dogwoods
sport necklaces like blood droplets in the green.

Whispers underfigure the rush, constant under
twitter, hoot, and chitter of birds. Leaf whisper,
whisper of edge-lap on leaf-fall, whisper of little lights
that skitter and dance on water.

Constant motion stirs up green scents, mold musk,
tang of water on limestone, notes of moss and
loam, pitch pine evergreen, raw alchemy,
perfume and balm.

The Farmer's Son Begs Relief

Cows, placid in the gloaming, like lilies
neither worry nor toil, live all their lives
in cycles of the udder, the breast, full or slack,
a calf attached, or a machine, or a hand to drain
milk, the life that flows through, returns to earth,
to the pasture in streams of piss, hot and yellow.
All flows through the breast as she grazes and mothers,
bawls for relief from the thing that strains her breast.

The cancer eats his mother, eats his childhood,
eats his innocence. The thing that eats his mother
confounds him. Will it consume his mother whole
or will she fight it off? He cannot help her,
he cannot help himself. They are dependent
upon the skill of strangers and their machines and
their hands. Must trust people who are not their people
to relieve the thing that strains her breast.

Changeling

When sorrow comes to your bed
like a just-weaned child, remember
sharp teeth and an appetite too large
to succor. It has its own bed, its own
place, so you both rest, so in the light
of day you give it what it needs,
not what it wants.

It may have the face of love
but sorrow thinks only
of itself, wails in the dark
where it must learn to sleep.

Eclipse

On the grassy bank beneath the MedFlight pad,
radiation techs, doctors, nurses, and clerical staff hold
solar glasses and homemade viewers—high tech and low.
Some in scrubs, others in hospital gowns, all convene
to view the eclipse. Appointed time, I go, beam-treated,
rejoin the group. The next patient wipes tears
on her gown sleeve as they help her walk.
All come back, light dims, trees cast
slivered shadows, a cardboard viewer shows a tiny image
of a giant sun, a colander throws a hundred moon-eaten
suns to the pavement.

Temperature drops,
light silvers and winks out, we gasp as one,
a pause in the world.

Solstice

Winter's woods wait, neither bleak nor bare.
Subtle hues with flares of neon moss,
limbs tipped with blushed buds wait lengthened days,
damp stone, curly lichens follow watery north light.
Winter-darkened deer paw tanned and wizened leaves
for buried shoots and ferns. Dark cedars sport ornaments
of cardinals and jays. Birds flit in the weak gloaming
that flushes, then bruises,
fades to shadow and sparkle
under an icy moon.

Bird Boy
for the colonel, 1969–2013

Your letters remain. Binary bits archived in wires,
chips, the cloud. Discussions of medicine, architecture,
martial arts, poetry. Confessions of astonishment at finding
love, wild and unbridled, an admission of adolescent
awkwardness in this thing, from this man, commander of many,
monolithic to others, my friend, butt of my jest and ribbing.

The tangible remains. Your dog tags, my poetry
you carried in the field, annotated with comments,
questions I never got to answer. A feather and stone,
talismans I sent, came back to me, and your cherished
Gaelic Bible and childhood books, my inheritance.
A morale patch, an enameled egg from Kandahar,
a copy of Hopkins, annotated and questioned,
and a translation of Lorca inscribed with a birthday greeting
in your microscopic script, signed with your nickname, a gross
contradiction to your other life, golden eagles on your shoulders.

The *letter home* remains. A recording of your profound voice
that could call down God. I count feathers I find,
enough to fledge a flock of birds. You said they would
come to me as a sign of you. Though fewer fall now,
they still come as omens and portents.

Your walking heart remains. Wild grief tempered
to sudden gnash of teeth, leashed but not tamed.
A bird on the wing, flown south from your river valley,
drops a feather. You are here.

Walking the Wilderness Road
at Cumberland Gap

The government tore up a road, put in a walking trail,
restored the Wilderness Road. I remember
a painting of Daniel Boone and his caravan
in my Tennessee history book;
worn, grim, and determined, those settlers
strode this very path across Virginia to Kaintuck—
the dark and bloody ground of the Shawnee.
At trail entrance, concrete sidewalks appear
rough and unfinished but feature hundreds
of animal tracks—bison, bear, bobcat—horseshoes,
wagon wheels, booted prints, and bare human feet.
A tunnel-like shed funnels walkers onward.
From above, recordings of game calls, footsteps, hoofbeats,
oxen, and clatter of wagons. To each side, rusty statuary stands,
featureless outlines of long-forgotten dreams
onto forested path, gives way to clearings where
meadowsweet and black cohosh bloom. Creek courses
by willow, sycamore, and gravel root growing tall
on marshy banks, all in pharmacopoeias of gone days
and I am lulled to a time of ago. I see another's feet below me
trudging that road to uncharted lands, determined to pass
forest unscathed, to better places.
I sense, then smell a musk of black energy

on high ridgeline, feel the dark move on padded paws
and I turn back to present, pick up my pace
to trailhead and we move on, move on.

Buick Reverie

I saw my mother's car today—
a sand-colored Buick that drove and rode like a boat,
an old-folks car, all leather, all automatic, full chrome.
Her hope to drive again stillborn in ICU after the crash that
left her unconscious for days. Reflexes too slow for traffic,
we cruised the parking lots of closed stores
until she realized her worst truth. Ministrokes,
A-fib, and medications wrecked her independence.

I piloted that craft four or five times a week
to doctor after doctor, the grocery, unending
Walmart trips where she still raced the aisles
in her motored cart, and on her penultimate day,
I struggled her chair from the car into the heart center
where they attached monitors that summoned an ambulance
to her home when she stroked out the next day.

The man who owns the Buick lives across the ridge—
five miles of curvy country roads wind between.
Once a mechanic, he bought it without haggling,
declared that engine model a miracle
of longevity. The exchange paid the legal fee
to settle her estate, finalized a life.

I followed and remembered as we navigated
the back roads toward the highway.
At the intersection, we turned opposite ways,
the taillights flashed and her car sailed away.

Menagerie

I gathered a list of heart words, gleaned from poems
teacher read us, road signs, Sunday school cards,
the *True Romance* magazines Mama didn't know
I could read, from cereal boxes, seed catalogs,
National Geographic, and *TV Guide*. On Thursdays,
I aced the *Reader's Digest* vocabulary quiz
while Mama shopped and I sat on the lower
edge of the magazine rack in Kroger.

The spiral-bound tablet from my uncle's store
spilled into the next tablet, into the next. At seven,
words followed me like stray dogs, jumped into
my lap until petted: *azure, cerulean, cerise, fulsome,*
frigate, hazard, rapture, dappled, exaltation, minion, and
my best pet, *vermilion.* Many I knew on the page,
sounds unfamiliar until I met the spoken version years later.

Words cavorted and pranced as my verse-loving
teacher paraded them daily. I studied their shapes and spelled
them all the way to Knoxville, a champion. The words assembled for
my amusement as the tablets gave way to notebooks of poems,
menageries of words, my companions and confidantes.

First Morning

Insects whir me awake, the curtains blow in,
tickle my face, crape myrtles scratch my
screen window, the breeze already hot, stirs and fails.
In the kitchen, coffee and oatmeal wait;
I should not, but will, drink the dark brew.
The neighbor leaves a dusty wake on our
gravel road, faint snatches of song
from Mama's radio surface like bubbles on a pond.
My nose drips, throat scratches with ragweed,
but I bounce up, anxious, tidy hair and face,
bind my ponytail just so, find my favorite new dress.
Crape myrtles mean August.
August means school.
School means books and chalk, lined blue paper,
rules I understand, refuge where I perform to standard.
Each plastered room painted, above and below,
two bland institutional colors, this room pink and tan.
Rows of carved and lettered wooden desks,
green chalkboards, oiled wooden floors, two tables,
six full bookcases, a good sign. A parade of presidents
tops one chalkboard where the date, August 21, 1962, presides.
On each desk waits a *Weekly Reader*. A bell clatters,
we rise, pledge, and begin.

Acknowledgments

Many thanks to the publications that first shared these poems. A big thank you to Lisa Parker, who never hesitated to take a pen to earlier iterations of this work. To my devoted readers and critics Melanie Hutsell, Dr. Kellie Brown, and Sylvia Woods, I give never-ending thanks. Jennifer Miller, thanks for your help in suggesting an order to the chaos. So many of these poems were written in response to prompts given by the wonderful, one and only Bill Brown, workshop leader extraordinaire. Sincere thanks to Drs. Devapiran Jaishankar, Elizabeth Lawson, and Kyle Colvett for their efficient and kind treatment and for keeping me here on this planet. I want to thank the University Press of Kentucky's Ashley Runyon and Patrick O'Dowd. To Silas House, my editor, many thanks; who would have thought we'd end up here?

Publications

A! Magazine for the Arts: "The Time I Stole"

Appalachian Review (formerly *Appalachian Heritage*): "Safety of Small Things," "Changeling," "Agent of Providence"

Appalachian Places: "Night Music," "Drawn," "Closed Hold," "Pyburn Creek," "Communion," "Persist," "Follow," "Take This Leaf," "Abscission"

Asheville Poetry Review: "Eclipse," "Ode on an Onion"

HeartWood: "This Morning, in the Mist"

In God's Hand anthology (Grace Writers, 2017): "An East Tennessee Parking Lot," "Longing"

Kudzu: "Pocket Money," "Persimmons"

Pine Mountain Sand & Gravel: "PTSD," "Buick Reverie"

Still: The Journal: "Birthday, 1956," "Shadows"

Women Speak, volume eight (Sheila-Na-Gig Editions, 2022): "What I Learned," "Tobacco," "Spotlight"